NEERAJ CHOPRA

ATTITUDE IS EVERYTHING

ANKIT CHAUHAN

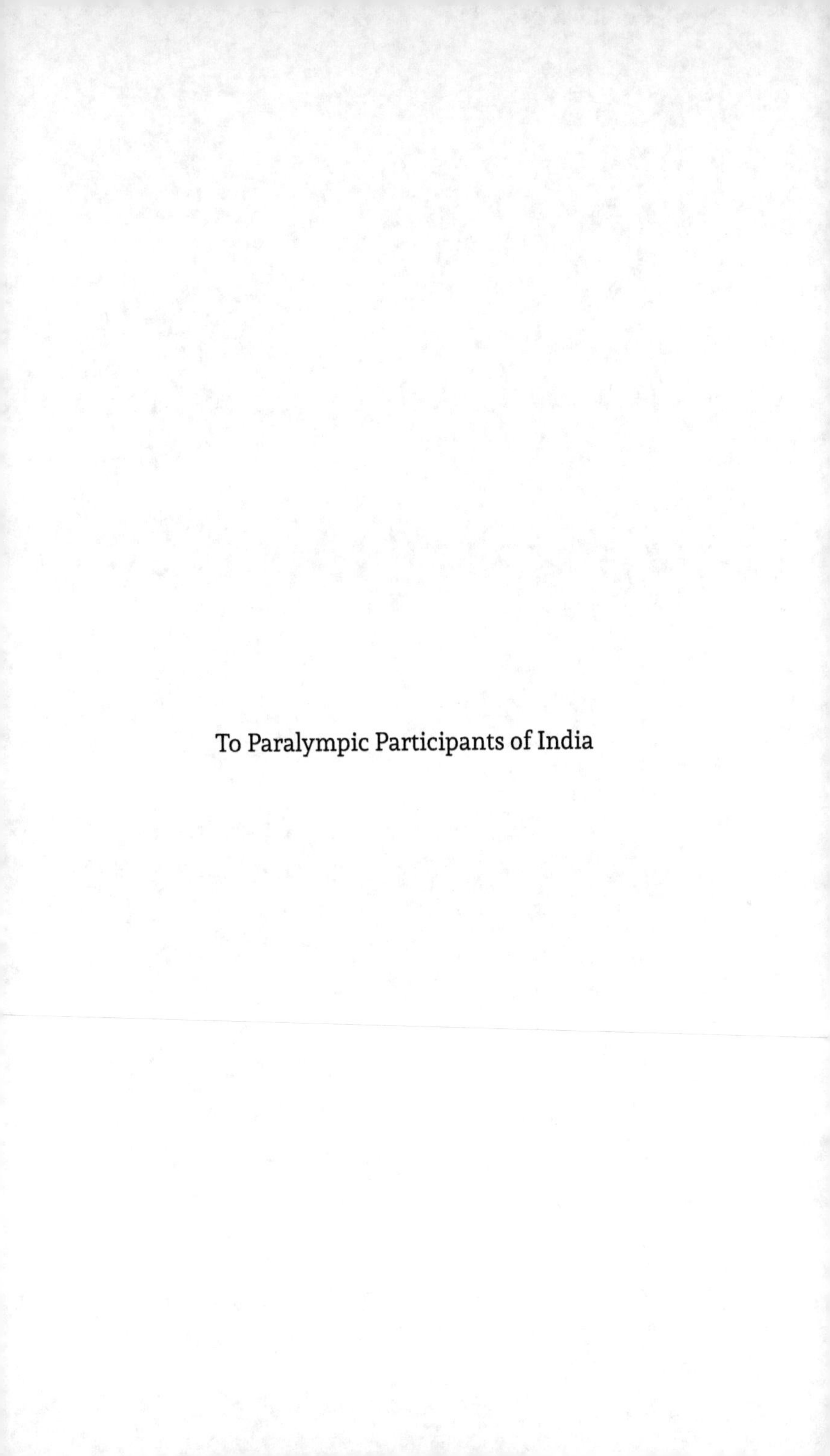

To Paralympic Participants of India

Contents

PREFACE

What's Unstoppable Attitude?

Everyone of us faces the setbacks in life and we stop continue to follow our dreams due to some of the major setbacks. You feel so low, that nothing seemed to make you happy? No matter how hard you tried, you just felt like the world was against you. Often when we're caught in an unhappy situation, we feel limited and sometimes trapped. We want to get out of it as quickly as we can, but it's never quite that simple.

"Whatever it may be, could you recall how your attitude was towards that situation?"

Your attitude determines how you interpret what events mean. Take obstacles, for example. Everyone who pursues any goal will inevitably run into obstacles. Your attitude determines what those obstacles mean and therefore how well you deal with them.

Unstoppable Attitude means Positive way to perceive all situations, use of positive words, Conscious, Committed to go ahead, going beyond comfort zone, clarity in visualisation and being around positive people.

It ensures that any setback you might encounter will not stop you or change your state of mind, and that you will go on, try again, and do your best despite any setbacks.

Every step that you take , every attempt that you make , success is always there. One just needs to look for it . Success need not be covered in silver or decorated with gold, it can be there in a simple platter . Whether you accept it or not is up to you.

ACKNOWLEDGEMENTS

I would like to thank Almighty God for giving me all the inspiration that gives me power to write this wonderful book in His words. I'd also like to thank the many people whose journey became part of the book itself that speaks through words.

Additionally, my special thanks to Bhushan Khairnar, my mentor and business analyst guiding me on every step about writing my first book. we have always wanted to contribute to the growth and unstoppable, unmatched success from this book.

An additional thanks to my parents, my mother for always being the person I could turn to during those dark and desperate years. She sustained me in ways that I never knew that I needed. To my younger brother, Aakash, and my father, Guddu Singh who always had faith and trust in me, thank you for letting me know that you had nothing but great memories of me. To my friends, they all may be batshit crazy, but even if I got to choose, I'd still choose to be with you all.

Finally, I would like to thank my wife, Priyanka, for tolerating my incessant disappearances and time that she always deserve. She kept me motivating me, instead writing this amazing geek till late night. A lifelong partner makes the life journey and destination worthwhile.

PROLOGUE

Your attitude has a significant impact on your likelihood of success in all parts of your life. Your thoughts, words and actions each have a unique impact on your success. Unstoppable Attitude can be achieved through appropriate mental approach and actions that we take.

1) *Your Attitude towards Circumstances:*

You might be in favourable or unfavourable situation. It's YOU who decide how is your attitude towards the situation and act accordingly. Your attitude toward your life and the people around you is your window to the world. If you think you can do something, then you can. If you think you can't, then you can't. You're right either way, as your attitude will impact your outcomes. It's the classic self-fulfilling prophecy. So try to change your attitude to one that is more positive. Our thoughts dominate and drive our circumstances.

2) *Positive Filter and Negative Filter:*

Attitude has filters through which we experience the world. Some of us see the world through a Positive Filter, while others perceive the world through a Negative Filter. Some people see the glass as half full and some as half empty. We have power to choose whether to see the situation, things and world though Positive attitude or Negative Attitude.

To illustrate this point, let's compares attitudes to windows. Your window is your perspective on the world. We all start with a clean window when we are young. But with age, our window gets covered in dirt from everything life throws at us: criticism, ridicule, rejection and disappointment.

This dirt is what makes us doubt our capabilities. Doubt feeds negative attitudes. Our job is to keep our view of the world clean. In other words, try to keep a positive attitude. Use a filter of optimism instead of negativity. Instead of saying "I can't," you should be saying "I can." Then, when your window is clean, you can finally see the world outside is full of positive opportunities.

If we can choose our attitude toward our circumstances, we can also choose all our reactions and responses.

3) Thoughts are Reflection of our Life:

On a basic level, we are human magnets. Thoughts means how we perceive the world and how we process the information - in negative light or positive light. It's about our Habit of thinking. If we have positive habit of thinking, the success will follow. We become what we think about.

Let's introduces the idea of "dominant thought." Dominant thoughts are outcome of our attitude. Your dominant thoughts rule the day. If you continually think positively about a goal, you will take steps to move toward that goal. But with a negative attitude, you are never going to take that first step. If we are always thinking negatively, we will produce "negative" actions. These are actions that don't move us toward our goals.

So you must choose consciously your positive thoughts. Think positive thoughts until it becomes a habit. Your beliefs brought you to where you are today. The way you think about things from this point on will determine your path forward.

One way to change your thinking is to become aware of what you say to yourself. You can also read positive literature daily and listen to motivational programs. Repetition is the key.

Expecting overnight success is a dangerous approach to embracing positive thoughts. We can be positive as often as possible, but that does not mean we should expect instant success.

4) *The Power of Visualization:*

Visualization is something we use to understand our circumstances. You have used visualization from a young age, and you should continue to use it. We shall always create mental movies in their minds, picturing every milestone toward the ultimate goal we want to achieve.

You must also rid your mind of old mental images that remind you of negative factors, like failure and disappointment. If you are still failing, then you are still holding on to pictures of lower aspiration or failure. Let's talk about the story of singer Celine Dion as an example. From the age of 5, she imagined herself singing in front of a vast audience and receiving multiple awards. She continued to hold onto these positive images throughout her life, and she ultimately accomplished living her dreams.

5) *Commitment*

Our frontal lob is designed to predict future and based on that we take actions. And to become Action Committed, we shall ask ourself whether we are willing to do whatever it takes to accomplish our objective.

The key to getting what you want is this willingness to do whatever it takes. So make this commitment to yourself. Once you have supplied this commitment, you will then be determined to reach your goal. Positive events will also start happening once you have committed. People around you will start helping you to achieve your goal. It won't be easy, but if you don't give up, you can move mountains. Benjamin Roll, who at age 74 finally passed the California bar exam. He never gave up on his goal and finally cleared the exam on his fourteenth attempt.

6) *Failure is the Process:*

Failure checks our attitude. How you react when faced with problems and setbacks is vitally important. Generally, people start questioning themselves, their circumstances and their luck. After this initial disappointment, though, you have a choice to make. You either:

Keep feeling miserable OR Learn a lesson from the setbacks and move on. You can either dwell on the negative or find the lesson in a problem. Often "problems" aren't even real problems. Instead, they're merely opportunities to take positive action. They allow you to improve and do better next time. Adversity encourages us to make the necessary changes in our lives and to tap into our hidden potential.

Failures also give us perspective. Failures teach us to be grateful when small, positive things happen. Napoleon, who is quoted as saying, "Every adversity carries with it the seed of an equivalent or greater benefit."

7) *Choices of the Words that we Use:*

Words have immense power. Words can build your future, destroy your opportunities, or maintain the status quo. Your choice of words will define your personality. Thoughts lead to Feelings, Feelings lead to Actions, and Actions lead to Results.

"Words –> Beliefs –> Actions –> Results."

Since our Words ultimately lead to our Actions and Results, we must use our words carefully. If you use your words to put yourself down, this strengthens your pessimistic beliefs. Your beliefs become more negative, and this will stop you from taking positive action. So, you must use positive self-talk as often as possible and discuss your goals only with supportive people.

8) Relaxing in Comfort Zone:

96% of the people, they feel nice about being in comfort zone. If you want to be successful, you must be willing to be uncomfortable. To achieve your goals, you have to step out of your comfort zone. The people who succeed are those who overcome obstacles along the way, and you have to stretch yourself to improve.

This advice might sound simple, but most people still back away from scary situations and avoid taking action. Yet sometimes, scary challenges help you move closer to your goals. So you occasionally have to face your fears.

Backing away from things you fear also has negative consequences. Backing away will only lower your self-esteem, making you feel powerless and frustrated. Realize that you are sabotaging your success by avoiding difficult situations.

Always adopt a can-do attitude as you prepare to take on tough challenges. Doing this will help give you the courage to take on challenges and overcome life's obstacles. Repetition is vital because taking on one obstacle will make the next one easier to overcome.

I
Your Attitude towards Circumstances

Life Incident from Neeraj Chopra's Life:

Neeraj is not an exception. He faced the series of failures just like us - failure to qualify for the Olympics in 2016 and then making the cut at the junior Worlds mere days after the deadline for qualification had ended, rankles. So does missing out on qualification for the final at the Worlds and a missed opportunity for a medal at the Diamond League final and the IAAF Continental Cup. "At Zurich [in the Diamond League finals], I missed it by a whisker (0.03 metres). At the Continental Cup, the rules had changed."

Unstoppable Attitude Towards Circumstances:

A distinguishing characteristic of consistently successful people is their ability to maintain a positive and proactive attitude. Successful people think differently than average people. Successful people produce better outcomes because their R Factor is guided by a positive and proactive mindset. Their mind is not cluttered or distracted by pessimism, negativity, or cynicism; as a result, they are able to focus all of their mental energy on exploring solutions, taking effective action, and learning how to get better.

Attitude is the way you look at life. It is the way you choose to see and respond to events, situations, people, and yourself. Your attitude is not something that happens to you. You choose your attitude. Your attitude is created by your thoughts, and you choose your thoughts. You are the architect of your frame of mind. You decide how you will perceive and process the events of life and work. You make the decision if your mindset is positive or negative. If you want to feel better you have to think better. In order to be positive in the way you feel, it is necessary to be disciplined in the way you think.

A positive attitude is the result of a disciplined and deliberate way of seeing, thinking, and responding to life. It is a mental discipline. It is intentional. It is mental toughness. A positive attitude is not naïve, and it does not sugarcoat problems. Rather, it sees and acknowledges problems and then focuses on finding solutions and opportunities. It looks for the opportunity within the problem. A positive attitude is habit-forming, and it has an impact on you and people around you. A positive attitude affects you physically. A person with a positive attitude will almost always outperform a person with a negative attitude.

A negative attitude is the result of negative thinking. It is a lack of mental discipline. It focuses on the problem and stops looking for solutions or opportunities. A negative attitude can only survive on a steady diet of negative thinking and negative self-talk. A negative attitude is habit-forming, and it has an impact on you and the people around you. A negative attitude affects you physically. A person with a negative attitude will almost always lose to a person with a positive attitude. Sadly, many people with a negative attitude are stuck in a doom loop because they have a negative attitude about improving their attitude. This is not a good place to be!

Many years ago two salesmen were sent by a British shoe manufacturer to Africa to investigate and report back on market potential.

The first salesman reported back, "There is no potential here - nobody wears shoes."

The second salesman reported back, "There is massive potential here - nobody wears shoes."

This simple short story provides one of the best examples of how a single situation may be viewed in two quite different ways - negatively or positively.

We could explain this also in terms of seeing a situation's problems and disadvantages, instead of its opportunities and benefits.

When telling this story its impact is increased by using exactly the same form of words (e.g., "nobody wears shoes") in each salesman's report. This emphasises that two quite different interpretations are made of a single situation.

Here's how it works: Your attitude begins with what you choose to focus on and the words you use to express your focus. A person with an default-driven, negative mindset will focus on a situation and say something like, "That's a stupid idea. It will never work."

A person with a discipline-driven, positive mindset will look at the same situation and say something like, "That's an idea. I'm not sure if it will work, but let's explore it further and find out." Note carefully the difference in language between these two mindsets.

The default way of thinking uses phrases like "never" and "always." The disciplined way of thinking uses language like "possible" and "maybe" and "explore." Because attitude is so immediately responsive to language, the negative words will trigger negative feelings, and the positive words will trigger positive feelings.

Bit of Mind Work:

1. *Write couple of failure moments.*
2. *What did you think about your failures- reasons for failure or why you couldn't make it?*
3. *Write about recent failure and plan for the next small step of growth. Take a small step to move ahead. Don't plan for the big leap. Growth is steady and slow.*

II

Positive Filter and Negative Filter

Neeraj in Non-Favourable Circumstances:

It was also a period when the villagers and his peers had given him a nickname of 'Sarpanch' due to the kurta-pyjama that he wore as an overweight teenager. "Then I started running and losing weight. At that time, I would run a lot of races on the streets. I used to call my friends to do the same and they used to refuse. Now I go back and I get told by my friends that they wish that they had also done the same," he said.

'Sarpanch', however, has been long forgotten and has been replaced by a more prominent name. Having watched videos of champion thrower Jan Zelezny on YouTube, 'Zelezny' will be welcomed back with much fanfare.

His long hair has spawned another name now among some – 'Tiger'. His mother, who calls him 'Nijju' may ask him to cut his hair when he goes back home. His grandmother has another demand that Neeraj study further. "I won't. When I was young,

• 5 •

the school was in one direction and the playing field another way. I was the type that would do just enough to study for the exams."

When it comes to how we view the world, most of us fall into one of two categories: optimist or pessimist. And according to experts, whatever category you fall into has a lot to do with your upbringing.

"Optimism is a mindset that enables people to view the world, other people and events in the most favourable, positive light possible. Some people describe this as the 'half glass full' mentality," says Dr. Aparna Iyer, psychiatrist and assistant professor at the University of Texas Southwestern Medical Centre. "Optimists do acknowledge negative events, but they are more likely to avoid blaming themselves for the bad outcome, inclined to view the situation as a temporary one and likely to expect further positive events in the future."

"While some people may be unable to deal with uncertainty, positive individuals are able to adapt and thrive. Accept what you can and cannot control in the situation," says Hershenson. "For example, if you lose your job you cannot control the fact that you were fired or laid off. You can control whether you take steps to find a new job as well as whether you take care of yourself with proper nutrition and sleep."

Practicing mindfulness is a great way to help combat the tendency to ruminate over daily stressors, which is a breeding ground for negativity.

Just ask corporate giant Michael Eisner, former Walt Disney Company CEO, how he became so successful, and in a heartbeat, he'll say optimism. In his book, Work in Progress, Eisner says he has been upbeat for as far back as he could remember. As a kid, he went to New York Giants football games with a firm belief that they would win. In those days the team was mediocre at best, and by the fourth quarter they'd usually be down by four or five touchdowns. When his friends would want to leave early to beat the crowds out of the stadium, Eisner insisted on staying, responding, "The Giants have to score four times and get a field goal, but there are five minutes left, and they're going to do it." Even though the team invariably lost, Eisner would come back a few weeks later, certain the Giants would win. It was this kind of irrepressible optimism that propelled Eisner into the highest ranks of some of the most successful companies in the world.

1. "From my experience, optimism is both a personality trait and a product of our environment," says Karol Ward, LCSW, a licensed psychotherapist. "From an early age, babies and children pick up the emotional vibes in their homes. If the atmosphere is relaxed and loving, children blossom even if they innately have a tendency towards anxiety. But if the home environment is tense and filled with dysfunction, optimism is one of the first things to go. It's hard to be emotionally open and hopeful when that is not being modeled for you by your caretakers."

"For my clients who have historically tended to be pessimistic, they habitually view things as negative. I will ask them to challenge themselves to always consider that there may be another way of looking at things," says Iyer. Experts refer to the tactic as "positive reframing."

"For example, if a client expresses that an entire day was ruined because it was dark or rainy outside, I would challenge him to focus on what may have been gained during that time. Often, he will reply that he did end up spending time indoors relaxing, reading or cuddling up to somebody he loves. Instead of looking at events in the most negative possible light, I encourage clients to make an active effort to 'try on' positive lenses as much as possible. After a while, this will become effortless, a more automatic and optimistic frame of mind."

2. Two old friends met at a local social gathering and one was struck with how sad and depressed the other was.

"You look like your world is about to end," said Jack.

With a sad face, Joe replied, "You don't know the half of it. Three weeks ago, an aunt of mine died and left me $100,000."

"That's terrific!" Jack said.

Scarcely pausing, Joe added, "Two weeks ago, this cousin I never heard of died, and I was his closest relative, so the lawyer said I'd inherited $95,000, all tax free."

"So why is that bad?"

"Then last week a grandfather I haven't spoken to in 10 years passed away, and he left me almost half a million dollars!"

"So what's your problem?"

"This week – nothing!"

You just can't please everyone.

I'm an eternal optimist. Where there is an optimist, there is a way. Success requires irrepressible optimism.

It's important to remember that making an effort to be more optimistic doesn't mean walking around wearing rose-colored glasses. While it's good for our mental health to see the positive in situations, not acknowledging the negative can hinder you in the long run.

"Optimism can be detrimental if it keeps you locked into fantasy and you are in denial about your current reality. You may be optimistic about finding a more lucrative job or loving relationship, but if you do not address the issues that are keeping you from those goals, you will not be able to create what you want," says Ward. "A combination of optimism and realistic thinking help people navigate through life. Realistic thinking does not mean never seeing the bright side of life; not at all. It is simply a way of supporting your optimism with the action steps so that you can create a positive future as opposed to being stuck in fantasy."

Bit of Mind Work:

1. *What are the negative comments that you receive from your family and friends?*
2. *How do you respond to it?*
3. *Plan - How will you convert the negative into positive? Describe.*

III

Thoughts are Reflection of our Life

Neeraj Chopra's Thought to Success:

"There should be gradual progression," is Chopra's advice for budding athletes. "Athletes should first think of the Nationals, then international meets, then the Asian, Commonwealth Games and after all that, the Olympics. Sometimes, athletes think of the final goal and end up over-training and injuring themselves, or consuming something they shouldn't have."

There's a 'secret' that all great historical and present thinkers, philosophers, and high achievers have agreed to be a universal truth.

This secret revolves around this simple idea: You are what you think.

English philosopher James Allen wrote: "As a man thinks, so he is; as he continues to think, so he remains." Stoic and Roman emperor Marcus Aurelius wrote: "A man's life is what his thoughts make of it." Poet and philosopher Ralph Waldo Emerson wrote: "A man is what he thinks about all day long." Author Earl Nightingale said: "We become what we think about," and Mark Twain wrote: "Life consists mainly of the storm of thoughts that is forever flowing through one's head." So, you have more influence with others if you can influence what they think, and have them thinking about that more often too. Get others thinking about it all the time and you have created a Dominant Thought.

Most of us must have heard this old saying "What you think about, you bring about." In fact, our thoughts create our reality. Everything that we experience in our life originates from our dominant thoughts. We can become the master of our life by becoming aware of our thought patterns, by controlling the nature of our dominant thoughts and by replacing our negative, unwanted thoughts with more positive ones which are in alignment with what we want to manifest in our physical world.

Our dominant thoughts can either be positive or negative and whether our thoughts are positive or negative our mind will always act on them and we will as a result experience the corresponding situation in our life. If our dominant thoughts are positive, we will have a more positive life. However, if our dominant thoughts are negative, we will attract more negative experiences in our life. As James Allen, author of "As a man thinketh" rightly said "A man's mind may be likened to a garden, which may be intelligently cultivated or allowed to run wild; but whether cultivated or neglected, it must, and will, bring forth. If no useful seeds are put into it, then an abundance of useless weed seeds will fall therein, and will continue to produce their kind."

If you have children, think back to when you or your partner was pregnant, and in the middle of the pregnancy with your first child. When you went out of the house back then, did you see more baby buggies as you walked your neighbourhood? Yes, and over your breakfast each morning did you tell your partner "Let's go look for baby buggies today?". No, right? You see, you were always thinking about the baby (a dominant thought), and a thought with lots of emotion attached to it, so your sub-conscious mind kept pointing out everything connected with that thought...the baby buggies. Now, that's powerful.

As I was practicing brushing with my left hand, I noticed something interesting happening. My dominant right hand would hover involuntarily near my chest or face, ready to take over in an instant. Sometimes, I would switch to the right hand without even realising it. It would happen so fast that there was no conscious decision making involved.

With my brushing, I taught my mind to watch out for the right hand creeping up or taking over. With that came a working circuit in my brain that was triggered, to remind me and to take counteractions.

The same applies when dealing with negative thoughts. Train yourself to become consciously aware of the dominant thought trying to take over. They are not going to just go away because you have replaced it with a good one. They only remain dormant, ready to take over at the most inopportune moment.

If you wire your brain to simultaneously remind you that it is happening and initiate a counter process, then you will be prepared — because this action too eventually will become a habit.

Bit of Mind Work:

1. *List the things about which you have negative thinking or you feel to run away from doing it?*
2. *Think - is this the way you always think about something?*
3. *List the things about which you are positive.*
4. *What other things that you can think positively about? List it.*

IV
The Power of Visualization

Life Incident from Neeraj Chopra's Life:

The gentle giant, who threw the spear to a distance of 87.58 metres to win gold, says, "This has never come to my mind. It's just my first Olympics. My focus is just javelin and nothing else. Let me write a few more chapters of my life and only then the director can think of a movie." - Neeraj After winning Olympic Gold Medal.

" Whatever we plant in our subconscious mind and nourish with repetition and emotion will one day become a reality".

– Earl Nightingale

If you're a very literal-minded or pragmatic person, you might have a healthy dose of skepticism about the power of visualisation. And indeed there are many who are not wrong in believing that visualising success often amounts to little more than a lazy substitute for actually doing something to make that success happen.

But visualisation is about much more than just sitting back and imagining that good things will happen. There is actually a huge body of research suggesting that mental imagery can dramatically impact our actions.

New research coming out of Oxford and Cambridge, for example, suggests that your ability to vividly imagine details about a bright future dramatically increases your energy and momentum, which leads, in turn, to constructive action. When our mind's eye can picture exactly what that bright future looks like, it can orient itself in the direction of what we envision.

You have goals. I know you do. Big dreams, deep longings, and an awareness that it is up to you to make them happen. Our subconscious mind processes things at a rate much higher than our conscious mind. The subconscious mind thinks in images and feelings, so you are much more likely to obtain a future goal if you try focusing on the images and feelings associated with them

All top performers, regardless of profession, know the importance of picturing themselves succeeding in their minds before they actually do in reality. Something I have been able to translate over to the business arena from athletics is the power of visualisation. It is extremely effective when harnessed and used correctly.

Consider these three examples:

Boxing legend Muhammad Ali was always stressing the importance of seeing himself victorious long before the actual fight.

** As a struggling young actor, Jim Carrey used to picture himself being the greatest actor in the world.*

** Michael Jordan always took the last shot in his mind before he ever took one in real life.*

Scientists working at the Wellcome Trust Centre for Neuroimaging at the Institute of Neurology in London have discovered that people who visualize a better future are more likely to be able to bring that future into existence. In the publication documenting their findings, the neurologists wrote: "The ability to construct a hypothetical scenario in one's imagination prior to it actually occurring may afford greater accuracy in predicting its eventual outcome."

What do you want to see? See yourself in the future. Picture a moment where your wish has already become a reality. What are you wearing? What time of year is it? Who is with you? How do you feel? Imagine every rich detail. The more vivid you can get, the better it will work for you.

Whatever your goal may be, take the time to visualize what life will be like once you've achieve it. "If your goal is to get a promotion at work, picture your boss calling you into their office and telling you about the raise or title change. Picture the increased salary going into your bank account or your new business cards with an updated title," Hershenson says. This is the outcome, and picturing it can give you a clear idea of where you're headed.

You are essentially putting the pin in the map of your destiny. You might even see details that you might strike you at first as funny or that you didn't even consciously know you desired, but because you pictured them your mind is now open to those possibilities.

When done correctly, this simple exercise can take your goals from being vague and seemingly impossible to achieve to being SO REAL you can literally see and feel them come to life.

Seeing is believing. When you can picture your future, your success, you are far more likely to take action towards your dreams and squash those negative thoughts that hold you back. Great athletes do it. Top performers do it. You can do it too.

Bit of Mind Work:

1. *Do you think the incident ahead of its happening in your imagination?*
2. *Bring clarity in your mind first - what best you can do rather to perform better than your competitor.*
3. *Visualise your next goal and write it down in your diary.*

V
Commitment

Neeraj Chopra's Commitment towards the Game: (Not towards the GOLD)

"I have a few years to go as an athlete. I want to win gold again in Paris 2024 and that will take a lot of hard work. Movies and all that can wait till I retire," says Neeraj Chopra, whose brand value has soared after his gold-winning feat.

"I am not a great fan of social media. It's a source of entertainment and I use it sometimes. Before the Tokyo Games, I was simply focusing on my preparation," says Chopra.

Commitment and Perseverance is that determination to follow something through until the end. It's playing until the final whistle and always doing your best, even when things seem to be going against you. It is the key to success. It often proves that you don't always have to be the smartest, the richest or the funniest person in the room, but you do have to learn to endure. When you practice perseverance in everything you do, you will start to build your natural endurance for seeing your way through difficult or challenging circumstances. As that natural endurance grows, you will start to feel the joy of hard work and overcoming difficult obstacles. It makes your successes that much sweeter. You will be proud of yourself.

No matter how blessed you are, life is always going to throw you curveballs. When you learn to persevere, who knows, you might even start looking forward to some of those curveballs. You never know when your hard work will tilt the balance and pay off, so you have to stay committed to those things that are most important to you.

Commitment is powerful. It makes the difference between failure and success at work, at school and at home. It affects how we feel about ourselves and how we feel about our relationships with others. When we fail on our commitments, our integrity and self-esteem are diminished, and others learn we cannot be trusted. We find ourselves making excuses and blaming others, distracting us further from the things we should be doing.

Be fully present when you commit to things, considering them carefully and thoughtfully in advance. Understand, as Murray wrote, once you're committed, you should not draw back. When you choose whether to commit, consider your ability and your time. Be specific about your commitment and seek to stretch yourself. Goal-setting researchers Edwin Locke and Gary Latham found that setting specific and challenging goals leads to higher performance 90 percent of the time.

Many years ago, a general landed his fleet on the enemy's shores. Prepared to wage a nasty battle, the fleet was outnumbered. The men knew that. So did the general.

But the general also knew that because they were outnumbered and their chances were slim to winning that battle, he needed to do something to get the mens' commitment.

He mulled it over for a few minutes, then made a brash decision. Lining the men up on the shore in front of the ships, he launched into a heated discourse.

Just before his long-winded speech to his men, he instructed his lieutenants to burn the ships. As he spoke, the ships went up in flames. He told the soldiers that there was now no retreat. Either they win or they perish there.

They won that battle against a superior enemy because there was no return. They'd burned the ships. The general knew that the desire for the men to see their families would win out their disadvantage on the battlefield.

And it worked.

If you're not ready or able to climb a mountain, then see if you can walk up a hill. If you're not ready to walk up a hill, then take a stroll.

If you're not able to take a stroll, then you can take a step. After taking that step, you might just find out you're ready to take another.

If you have trouble imagining yourself reaching your goal, then imagine yourself taking one small, simple action in the direction of that goal. Imagine it, and then, like the Nike commercials, just do it.

After that first step, there will be another one you can take, something that's a little bit more challenging and yet not overwhelming. Keep it up, and soon your ultimate goal begins to come into view.

We can accomplish anything if we are willing to keep taking the next step when it is time to do so. What we lack in brute strength, resources, knowledge or skills, we can make up for with commitment and persistence. We can absolutely get where we choose to go if we are committed.

We just need to be persistent and focused on the journey. There is no time like the present to get started.

Keep in mind that commitment, dedication and persistence is what allows us to turn challenges into successes.

Bit of Mind Work:

1. *Write down the things your are good at, the skills and activities.*
2. *Plan how you can become better about it.*
3. *Commit yourself to become better in what you are better at most.*

VI
Failure is the Process

Neeraj Chopra - Failure as a way to Success:

Chopra won gold in the 2017 Asian Athletics Championships with a throw of 85.23 metres. He then went to London in August for the World Championships, but was eliminated before reaching the finals. On 24 August, Chopra suffered a significant groin injury in the finals of the Zurich Diamond League, sustaining the injury during his third attempted throw, in which he attained a distance of 83.39 meters; owing to the injury, he fouled his fourth attempt and skipped his last two allowed attempts. His first and best throw of 83.80 meters gave him a seventh-place finish. As a result, he withdrew from competition for the remainder of 2017. After recovering from his injury, which he partly attributed to a heavy competition schedule and the lack of a proper diet and rest, Chopra spent a month at the Joint Services Wing sports institute in Vijayanagar. He then left for Offenburg, Germany in November to train for three months with Werner Daniels, whom he had briefly worked with before the 2017 World Championships. His former coach Calvert had left India in May due to disputes over his contract. During his stay in Offenburg, Chopra focused on strength training and honed his technique with Daniels' guidance, adjusting his stance and improving his range by keeping his hand raised higher during throws.

Failure is part of life, and most certainly part of business. We don't often acknowledge it, but failure is also a fundamental element of our success.

Our instinct is to be ashamed of failure, maybe because we don't like how it makes us feel--humiliated, as though we have done something wrong.

But if you can shift your perspective and look at failure not as something to be ashamed of but something valuable, you can begin to understand that it's through failure that we truly learn to succeed.

The sooner we stop shaming our failures, the easier it will be to turn them to our advantage.

Failures are the gifts that make us dig out and figure out who we are, what we're made for, and what we're responsible to give back to life." - Tony Robbins

Failure is fundamental to our growth. If we can learn from what went wrong and why we know what to avoid or alter in the future to avoid a repeat. Or as Bill Gates once put it: "Success is a lousy teacher. It seduces smart people into thinking they can't lose."

The wisdom of learning from failure is incontrovertible. Yet organisations that do it well are extraordinarily rare. This gap is not due to a lack of commitment to learning. Managers in the vast majority of enterprises that I have studied over the past 20 years—pharmaceutical, financial services, product design, telecommunications, and construction companies; hospitals; and NASA's space shuttle program, among others—genuinely wanted to help their organisations learn from failures to improve future performance. In some cases they and their teams had devoted many hours to after-action reviews, postmortems, and the like. But time after time I saw that these painstaking efforts led to no real change. The reason: Those managers were thinking about failure the wrong way.

Colonel Harland Sanders has become a world-known figure by marketing his Kentucky Fried Chicken. The story of Colonel Harland Sanders is an example of how perseverance, dedication, and ambition along with hard work can create success; regardless of your age.

At the age of sixty-five, after running a restaurant for several years, Harland Sanders found himself penniless. He retired and received his first social security check which was for one hundred and five dollars.

Harland Sanders was a man who really loved to share his fried chicken recipe. He had a lot of positive influence from those who tasted the chicken. Harland was retired, getting older and while most people believed in the sanctimony of retirement, Harland opted to sell the world on his cool new chicken recipe. Harland traveled door to door to houses and restaurants all over his local area. He wanted to partner with someone to help promote his chicken recipe. He was met with little enthusiasm.

He started travelling by car to different restaurants and cooked his fried chicken on the spot for restaurant owners. If the owner liked the chicken, they would enter into a handshake agreement to sell his chicken. He was turned down 1009 times before his chicken was accepted once!

By 1964, Colonel Harland Sanders had 600 franchises selling his trademark chicken. Now, he sold his company for $2 million dollars but remained as a spokesperson. In 1976, the Colonel was ranked as the world's second most recognizable celebrity.

"Inside of every problem lies an opportunity."

\- Robert Kiyosaki

While discussing inventions, Thomas Edison's associate, Walter S. Mallory, once said to him, "Isn't it a shame that with the tremendous amount of work you have done you haven't been able to get any results?"

Edison responded, with a smile, "Results! Why, man, I have gotten a lot of results! I know several thousand things that won't work."

People see success as positive and failure as a negative. Edison's quote shows that failure isn't a bad thing. You can learn, grow and evolve from your past mistakes. In business, failure is an all too common occurrence. After all, nine out of 10 small businesses will fail.

We can choose to see failure as "the end of the world," or as proof of just how inadequate we are. Or, we can look at failure as the incredible learning experience that it often is. Every time we fail at something, we can choose to look for the lesson we're meant to learn. These lessons are very important; they're how we grow, and how we keep from making that same mistake again. Failures stop us only if we let them.

It's easy to find successful people who have experienced failure. For example:

* *Michael Jordan is widely considered to be one of the greatest basketball players of all time. And yet, he was cut from his high school basketball team because his coach didn't think he had enough skill.*

* *Warren Buffet, one of the world's richest and most successful businessmen, was rejected by Harvard University.*

Richard Branson, owner of the Virgin empire, is a high-school dropout.

Most of us will stumble and fall in life. Doors will get slammed in our faces, and we might make some bad decisions. But imagine if Michael Jordan had given up on his dream to play basketball when he was cut from that team. Imagine if Richard Branson had listened to the people who told him he'd never do anything worthwhile without a high-school diploma.

Think of the opportunities you'll miss if you let your failures stop you.

Failure can also teach us things about ourselves that we would never have learned otherwise. For instance, failure can help you discover how strong a person you are. Failing at something can help you discover your truest friends, or help you find unexpected motivation to succeed.

Often, valuable insights come only after a failure. Accepting and learning from those insights is key to succeeding in life.

Bit of Mind Work:

1. *Write your one goal.*
2. *Describe the process in detail to achieve it.*
3. *Record what went wrong and right.*
4. *Repeat.*

VII
Choices of the Words that we Use

Life Incident from Neeraj Chopra's Life:

"We can't be satisfied with one gold, we need to think at a global level." Says Neeraj.

"Language shapes our behaviour and each word we use is imbued with multitudes of personal meaning. The right words spoken in the right way can bring us love, money and respect, while the wrong words—or even the right words spoken in the wrong way — can lead to a country to war. We must carefully orchestrate our speech if we want to achieve our goals and bring our dreams to fruition."

— Dr. Andrew Newberg, Words Can Change Your Brain

Words create worlds. Yes, your words. Much like God, who created everyone and everything with words, you also have the power to create with yours. The world you trod around in right now is the by-product of the words you tell yourself and the ones others tell you. Of course, only one physical world exists. But not everyone sees the same world. The world Jesus saw was radically different than the Pharisees, for example. Hitler's world was radically different than Martin Luther King's.

The same is true for you and me. We have the power to create the world we see with our words. We have the power to create the world other people see with our words.

The words you speak hold power. Power to create new possibilities or to close them down. Power to build relationships or to damage them. Power to lift people up or to pull them down. Yourself included.

We often don't realise just how impactful our words are – both on ourselves and others. If we did, we'd do far less complaining! You also would never hear yourself saying things like "It's impossible to…", "I'm totally hopeless at…" or "I had no choice…" – all phrases which undermine your own power and limit your future in some way, albeit unintentionally.

Psychologists have found that our subconscious mind interprets what it hears very literally. The words that come out of your mouth therefore create the reality you inhabit. For better or worse. Unfortunately it's often the latter as we unconsciously sabotage our success simply by using language that undermines our opinions, amplifies our problems and chips away at our confidence to handle them successfully.

Whatever direction your words lead, your mind, body and environment will follow. If you use positive language about yourself and your ability to learn new skills, achieve your goals and rise above difficulties, then that's what tends to show up externally. Likewise, if you're continually saying things that affirm incompetence, echo hopelessness, nurture anxiety or fuel pessimism, then that will also shape your reality. It may sound fanciful, but over time your world will morph to mirror your words.

It's therefore extremely important to be intentional about the words you use and speaking in ways that empower and expand rather than devalue and deflate.

The truth is that we possess far more power to affect positive change than we realise. Tapping in to that power starts with building self-awareness of where you are using what psychologists call "out of power" language.

Words are more powerful than you can imagine, so it is important to choose them wisely. They have the ability to carry us to far off, amazing places. Unfortunately, our words can also lead us to places we wish we had never visited.

Why? Words are a means for us to express and describe our experiences to others. So, they always have emotions attached to them. Our feelings are constantly creating our lives. The words we use, especially when spoken repeatedly, can deepen our feelings and ultimately become our experience.

If someone asks you how you are doing, do you respond with "I'm OK," or "I'm fine," or do you reply with "I'm feeling great!" or "Life is good!"? It may feel awkward at first to change your approach to words if they don't fit your typical routine or habit. But, it is well worth the effort, and will soon feel more natural.

As you shift to regularly using more positive words, you will feel better. Choose words that create happiness. Dwell on these words and the conversations around them.

View your ability to "create with words" as a natural wonder, giving you what you truly want in your life — more

joy!

Once you've started this positive journey, share your successes! When something wonderful happens to you, or you notice something positive happening around you, be sure to share it with others. Be quick to tell your family and friends by using words that express your appreciation for such a positive experience. Remember to share happy stories and good news often. When you come from a place of gratitude, others will be joyful with you.

So remember, although "choose your words wisely" may be a common phrase, following this advice can truly change your life. The words you must wisely choose will have a profound effect on your life experiences. Once you know and understand this connection between your heart and your words, you have the power to live a better life — one filled with more joy and abundance!

Bit of Mind Work:

1. *Observe your Whatsapp chat. Observe - How many words were positive and negative used by you.*
2. *Change he way you talk, if using negative words more. Improve step by step.*

VIII
Relaxing in Comfort Zone

The Pressure on Neeraj Chopra:

Neeraj said he did not feel too much pressure of being in the Olympics because he had competed with these men before. "The most important thing this year was to play competitions and I spoke to everyone and everyone supported me. The 2-3 international competitions I got was very important for me. It was the Olympics but it didn't feel like I had come to something new. I didn't feel pressure because I thought I have played with them and I could focus on my throw. The comeback from injury was great, it is my hard work but thank you to everyone."

The most sough sports celebrity of India. The cameras depict a confident young man throwing the javelin, yet the man from Khandra in Haryana is terrified of the cameras when asked to speak in front of them.

Become comfortable being uncomfortable. We always hear about stepping out of our comfort zone and pushing past our personal limits into some void of enlightenment. So is there a truth to all this?

People often spout it as motivation-- "Get out of your comfort zone!" they say, or, "Life starts when your comfort zone ends!"

But that begs the question, "Why?" Knowing why helps. Really think about things: Is it necessary?

The term comfort zone is a reference to our thoughts, our feelings, and our habits that contribute to our daily experience. This might also include the knowledge, skillset, and talents we have in life.

Let's start with this concept: Stepping out of one's comfort zone isn't always necessary. In general terms, we can build on our character strengths to create challenge and success in each unique venture.

Your comfort zone is where you live 90% of your life or more. You know how to get to work or wherever you have to go, you know how to pay the rent on time and pick out clothes to wear in the morning and so on. You know how to drive or take the bus or train. Normal life is not easy but you're well acquainted with almost every activity normal life requires of you.

Expanding your comfort zone is perhaps a better concept. It's an extension of your emotional limits, in order to reach one's full potential.

Expanding your comfort zone should not go against any clinical diagnosis of anxiety, phobias, or related mental conditions. Working through things like post-traumatic stress, depression, and generalised anxiety disorder requires the help from a mental health professional.

Our comfort zone is neither a good or bad thing. It's a natural state that most people trend towards. Leaving it means increased risk and anxiety, which can have positive and negative results (which we'll get to in a moment), but don't demonise your comfort zone as something holding you back. We all need that head-space where we're least anxious and stressed so we can process the benefits we get when we leave it.

Long time ago, a king received 2 beautiful baby eagles in form of a present.The king was very pleased with the gift and decided to hire an experienced caretaker for them.He took great care of them and developed such a strong bond with those two that they didn't need to be caged.

After few months the king decided to pay them a visit. He noticed that the 2 Babies had now developed into strong adolescents. The king wished to see them flying and ordered the caretaker to signal them to fly into the sky. On receiving his signal, both eagles began to fly. One of them flew high into the sky and touched new heights, While other one flew for some seconds and returned to the branch where it was earlier sitting.

King found this little weird and asked the caretaker that why is these two so contrasting. The caretaker told the king that this one had a problem from the beginning and he would never leave the branch.

The king desperately wanted the second bird to fly high as the first one. So he announced this as a challenge in his court and stated that the person who will be successful in making the eagle fly would receive a heavy prize from the king.

So, many scholars came and tried to apply the knowledge they had, but no one was successful. The king too lost hope and almost gave up

But after few days the caretaker informed the king that one man was successful in making the eagle fly high in the sky. He was then brought before the king where the king was eagerly waiting with the promised prize. The king learnt that the man was a simple farmer. He just asked him his method he used which lot of highly qualified people didn't think about.

He said," I simply cut the branch, the branch on which he had a habit of sitting. As there was no branch, he had no option but to fly other branches and which he did very well."

Friends, we all are meant to fly high in our life. But sometimes we underestimate ourselves and don't realise our true potential. We are habituated to doing certain things which will always limit us. Just as the eagle didn't realise that it could actually fly to number of branches he wished to as it always liked to remain on the same branch. After the farmer had cut it, it had no option but to expand its comfort zone and start working. Only then he realised its true potential.

Even we need to come out and expand our comfort zones as great things in life are only achieved by expanding comfort zone in which we keep living and hoping for life to get better

Your comfort zone can be a good place to be, as long as you don't tip the scales too far. It's important to remember there's a difference between the kind of controlled anxiety we're talking about and the very real anxiety that many people struggle with every day. Everyone's comfort zone is different, and what may expand your horizons may paralyse someone else. Remember, optimal anxiety can bring out your best, but too much is a bad thing.

Bit of Mind Work:

Here are some ways to expand your comfort zone without going too far:

** Do everyday things differently. Take a different route to work. Try a new restaurant without checking Yelp first. Go vegetarian for a week, or a month. Try a new operating system. Recalibrate your reality. Whether the change you make is large or small, make a change in the way you do things on a day-to-day basis. Look for the perspective that comes from any change, even if it's negative. Don't be put off if things don't work out the way you planned.*

** Take your time making decisions. Sometimes slowing down is all it takes to make you uncomfortable—especially if speed and quick thinking are prized in your work or personal life. Slow down, observe what's going on, take your time to interpret what you see, and then intervene. Sometimes just defending your right to make an educated decision can push you out of your comfort zone. Think, don't just react.*

** Trust yourself and make snap decisions. We're contradicting ourselves, but there's a good reason. Just as there are people who thrive on snap decisions, others are more comfortable weighing all of the possible options several times, over and over again. Sometimes making a snap call is in order, just to get things moving. Doing so can help you kickstart your personal projects and teach you to trust your judgement. It'll also show you there's fallout to quick decisions as well as slow ones.*

** Do it in small steps. It takes a lot of courage to break out of your comfort zone. You get the same benefits whether you go in with both feet as you do if you start slow, so don't be afraid to start slow. If you're socially anxious, don't assume you have to muster the courage to ask your crush on a date right away, just say hello to them and see where you can go from there. Identify your fears, and then face them step by* *step.*

When you plan something bigger, you must yourself ready for the pressure. Accept it as a part & partial towards the way to become Unstoppable Attitude.

About Author

Ankit Chauhan

Ankit is an innovation enthusiast and founder of Tolstoy World. He desire to bring best out of every young thinkers. The book is an effort to bring best within us. With the book, Ankit is debuting as Author.

Reference and Citations

- *In private in NYC and the author of the book: Borderline, Narcissistic, and Schizoid Adaptations. www.elinorgreenberg.com)*
- *https://focus3.com/the-power-of-attitude/*
- *https://www.linkedin.com/pulse/ 20140724045621-56724952-the-shoes-story-positive-thinking-negative-thinking-attitude-perspective-mindset*
- *https://www.nbcnews.com/better/health/how-train-your-brain-be-more-optimistic-ncna795231*
- *https://www.successwithcrm.com/blog/optimism-is-the-first-step-to-success*
- *https://www.markfritzonline.com/planting-and-watering-dominant-thoughts/*
- *https://www.omaritani.com/blog/what-you-think*
- *https://medium.com/illumination/how-to-get-positive-thoughts-to-stay-dominant-98fe5b241eee*
- *https://www.entrepreneur.com/article/242373*
- *https://www.wishbeads.com/blogs/wishbeads/true-story-power-visualization*
- *https://www.success.com/the-power-of-visualization/*
- *https://www.qualitymag.com/blogs/14-quality-blog/post/ 87753-commitment-and-persistence*
- *https://timgreenbooks.com/kids/commitment/*
- *https://www.characterlives.org/the-power-of-commitment/*
- *https://www.wanderlustworker.com/the-power-of-commitment/*
- *https://hbr.org/2011/04/strategies-for-learning-from-failure*
- *https://www.mindtools.com/pages/article/fear-of-failure.htm*

- *https://www.forbes.com/sites/lizryan/2016/09/03/ten-ways-to-expand-your-comfort-zone/?sh=7eb66aa49adf*
- *https://www.forbes.com/sites/lizryan/2016/09/03/ten-ways-to-expand-your-comfort-zone/?sh=401bd8db49ad*
- *https://lifehacker.com/the-science-of-breaking-out-of-your-comfort-zone-and-w-656426705*
- *https://medium.com/@BaysideChurch/words-create-worlds-some-thoughts-on-the-power-of-words-58c765aa173*
- *https://margiewarrell.com/your-words-create-your-reality/*
- *https://www.news-press.com/story/life/wellness/2014/02/25/life-coaching-choose-your-words-wisely-for-positive-effect/5788789/ Wasserman T, Wasserman L (2020). "Motivation: State, Trait, or Both". Motivation, Effort, and the Neural Network Model. pp. 93–101. doi:10.1007/978-3-030-58724-6_8. ISBN 978-3-030-58724-6. S2CID 229258237.*
- Caulton JR (2012). "The development and use of the theory of ERG: A literature review". Emerging Leadership Journeys. Regent University School of Global Leadership & Entrepreneurship. 5 (1): 2–8. CiteSeerX 10.1.1.1071.4400.
- Kazdin AE, ed. (2000). "Motivation: an overview". Encyclopedia of Psychology. American Psychological Association. ISBN 978-1-55798-187-5.
- Graham S. "Motivation". Encyclopedia of Education.
- Filipp SH. "Motivation". Encyclopedia of Aging.
- Mele AR (2005). "Motivation and Agency: Precis". Philosophical Studies. 123 (3): 243–247. doi:10.1007/s11098-004-4903-0. S2CID 143586904.
- Mele AR (2003). "7. Motivational Strength". Motivation and Agency. Oxford University Press.
- Mele AR (2003). "Introduction". Motivation and Agency. Oxford University Press.
- Miller C (2008). "Motivation in Agents". Noûs. 42 (2):

222–266. doi:10.1111/j.1468-0068.2008.00679.x.

- Wilson G, Shpall S, Piñeros Glasscock JS (2016). "Action". The Stanford Encyclopedia of Philosophy. Metaphysics Research Lab, Stanford University.
- Framarin CG (2008). "Motivation-Encompassing Attitudes". Philosophical Explorations. 11 (2): 121–130. doi:10.1080/13869790802015676. S2CID 143542576.
- Mele AR (2003). "7. Motivation and Desire". Motivation and Agency. Oxford University Press.
- Strandberg C (2012). "Expressivism and Dispositional Desires: 2. a distinction in mind". American Philosophical Quarterly. 49 (1): 81–91.
- Bartlett G (2018). "Occurrent States". Canadian Journal of Philosophy. 48 (1): 1–17. doi:10.1080/00455091.2017.1323531. S2CID 220316213.
- "Unconscious Motivation". Gale Encyclopedia of Psychology.
- Rueda R, Moll LC (1994). "Chapter 7: A Sociocultural Perspective on Motivation". In O'Neill Jr HF, Drillings M (eds.). Motivation: Theory and Research. Hillsdale, NJ: Lawrence Erlbaum Associates, Inc. ISBN 978-0-8058-1286-2.
- McCann H (1995). "Intention and Motivational Strength". Journal of Philosophical Research. 20: 571–583. doi:10.5840/jpr_1995_19.
- Broome J (2009). "Motivation". Theoria. 75 (2): 79–99. doi:10.1111/j.1755-2567.2009.01034.x.
- O'Connor T, Franklin C (2021). "Free Will". The Stanford Encyclopedia of Philosophy. Metaphysics Research Lab, Stanford University. Retrieved 13 May 2021.
- Ewing AC (1934). "Can We Act Against Our Strongest Desire?". The Monist. 44 (1): 126–143. doi:10.5840/monist19344415. ISSN 0026-9662. JSTOR 27901421.
- Pardee RL (1990). A literature review of selected theories dealing with job satisfaction and motivation. Motivation

Theories of Maslow, Herzberg, McGregor & McClelland (PDF) (Report). pp. 6–7. "The basic concept behind the hierarchy system is that it's like a food pyramid. Everybody starts at the bottom of the pyramid and is motivated to satisfy each level in ascending order to work our way to the top of the pyramid, and those levels (needs) are categorized into two main groups with five different sections which are explained below."

- *Crandall A, Powell EA, Bradford GC, Magnusson BM, Hanson CL, Barnes MD, Novilla ML, Bean RA (February 1, 2020). "Maslow's Hierarchy of Needs as a Framework for Understanding Adolescent Depressive Symptoms Over Time". Journal of Child and Family Studies. 29 (2): 273–281. doi:Schneider B, Alderfer CP (1973). "Three Studies of Measures of Need Satisfaction in Organizations". Administrative Science Quarterly. 18 (4): 489–505. doi:10.2307/2392201. JSTOR 2392201.*

- *Otundo JO, Garn A (2020-05-28). "Testing an Integrated Model of Interest Theory and Self-Determination Theory in University Physical Activity Classes". The Physical Educator. 77 (3). doi:10.18666/TPE-2020-V77-I3-9571. S2CID 219756118.*

- *Cooper JO (2007). Applied Behavior Analysis. Upper Saddle River, NJ, USA: Pearson Education. ISBN 978-0-13-129327-4.*

- *Schacter DL, Gilbert DL, Wegner DM (2009). Psychology (2nd ed.). New York: Worth.*

- *Deci EL, Koestner R, Ryan RM (November 1999). "A meta-analytic review of experiments examining the effects of extrinsic rewards on intrinsic motivation". Psychological Bulletin. 125 (6): 627–68, discussion 692-700. doi:Ryan RM, Deci EL (January 2000). "Intrinsic and Extrinsic Motivations: Classic Definitions and New Directions". Contemporary Educational Psychology. 25 (1): 54–67.*

CiteSeerX 10.1.1.318.808. doi:10.1006/ceps.1999.1020. PMID 10620381.

- Deci EL, Ryan RM (2013-06-29). *Intrinsic motivation and self-determination in human behavior*. New York. ISBN 978-1-4899-2271-7. OCLC 861705534.
- Deci EL (1971). "Effects of externally mediated rewards on intrinsic motivation". *Journal of Personality and Social Psychology*. 18 (1): 105–115. doi:10.1037/h0030644.
- Deci EL (1972). "Intrinsic motivation, extrinsic reinforcement, and inequity". *Journal of Personality and Social Psychology*. 22 (1): 113–120. doi:10.1037/h0032355.
- Graham S. "Motivation". *Encyclopedia of Education*.
- Wigfield A, Guthrie JT, Tonks S, Perencevich KC (2004). "Children's motivation for reading: Domain specificity and instructional influences". *Journal of Educational Research*. 97 (6): 299–309. doi:10.3200/joer.97.6.299-310. S2CID 145301292.
- Lowry PB, Gaskin J, Twyman NW, Hammer B, Roberts TL (2013). "Taking 'fun and games' seriously: Proposing the hedonic-motivation system adoption model (HMSAM)". *Journal of the Association for Information Systems*. 14 (11): 617–671. doi:10.17705/1jais.00347. SSRN 2177442.
- Parker CJ, Wang H (2016). "Examining hedonic and utilitarian motivations for m-commerce fashion retail app engagement". *Journal of Fashion Marketing and Management*. 20 (4): 487–506. doi:10.1108/JFMM-02-2016-0015.
- Yarborough C, Fedesco H (2020). "Motivating Students". *Vanderbilt University Center for Teaching*. Retrieved 4 March 2015.
- Donald JN, Bradshaw EL, Ryan RM, Basarkod G, Ciarrochi J, Duineveld JJ, Guo J, Sahdra BK (July 2020). "Mindfulness and Its Association With Varied Types of Motivation: A

Systematic Review and Meta-Analysis Using Self-Determination Theory". *Personality & Social Psychology Bulletin*. 46 (7): 1121–1138. doi:10.1177/0146167219896136. PMID 31884892. S2CID 209510306.

- Schroeder T (2020). "Desire". *The Stanford Encyclopedia of Philosophy*. Metaphysics Research Lab, Stanford University. Retrieved 22 May 2021.

- Reeve, Johnmarshall (2018). *Understanding motivation and emotion*. John Wiley & Sons. pp. 131–135. ISBN 978-1119367604.

- McClelland DC (1988). "1. Conscious and Unconscious Motives". *Human Motivation*. Cambridge University Press. pp. 3–30. doi:10.1017/CBO9781139878289.003. ISBN 978-0-521-36951-0.

- Freud S (2012). *A General Introduction to Psychoanalysis*. Renaissance Classics. ISBN 9781484156803.

- Deckers L (2018). *Motivation: Biological, Psychological, and Environmental*. Routledge. pp. 39–41. ISBN 9781138036338.

- Weingarten E, Chen Q, McAdams M, Yi J, Hepler J, Albarracín D (May 2016). "From primed concepts to action: A meta-analysis of the behavioral effects of incidentally presented words". *Psychological Bulletin*. 142 (5): 472–97. doi:10.1037/bul0000030. PMC 5783538. PMID 26689090.

- Bargh JA, Chartrand TL (2000). "Studying the Mind in the Middle: A Practical Guide to Priming and Automaticity Research". In Reis H, Judd C (eds.). *Handbook of Research Methods in Social Psychology*. New York, NY: Cambridge University Press. pp. 1–39.

- Elgendi M, Kumar P, Barbic S, Howard N, Abbott D, Cichocki A (May 2018). "Subliminal Priming-State of the Art and Future Perspectives". *Behavioral Sciences*. 8 (6): 54. doi:10.3390/bs8060054. PMC 6027235. PMID 29849006.

- "Mere Exposure Effect". *Encyclopedia of Psychology*.

2016-06-17. Retrieved 2018-10-13.

- Deckers L (2018). *Motivation Biological, Psychological, and Environmental* (5th ed.). 711 Third Avenue, New York, NY 10017: Routledge. pp. 30–38, 71–75. ISBN 9781138036321.

- Robbins TW, Everitt BJ (April 1996). "Neurobehavioural mechanisms of reward and motivation". *Current Opinion in Neurobiology.* 6 (2): 228–36. doi:10.1016/S0959-4388(96)80077-8. PMID 8725965. S2CID 16313742.

- Berridge KC, Kringelbach ML (June 2013). "Neuroscience of affect: brain mechanisms of pleasure and displeasure". *Current Opinion in Neurobiology.* 23 (3): 294–303. doi:10.1016/j.conb.2013.01.017. PMC 3644539. PMID 23375169.

- Salamone JD, Correa M (November 2012). "The mysterious motivational functions of mesolimbic dopamine". *Neuron.* 76 (3): 470–85. doi:10.1016/j.neuron.2012.10.021. PMC 4450094. PMID 23141060.

- Kennedy PJ, Shapiro ML (June 2009). "Motivational states activate distinct hippocampal representations to guide goal-directed behaviors". *Proceedings of the National Academy of Sciences of the United States of America.* 106 (26): 10805–10. Bibcode:2009PNAS..10610805K. doi:10.1073/pnas.0903259106. PMC 2705558. PMID 19528659.

- Southwood N (2016). "The Motivation Question". *Philosophical Studies.* 173 (12): 3413–3430. doi:10.1007/s11098-016-0719-y. S2CID 171181144.

- Broome J (2013). *Rationality Through Reasoning.* Wiley-Blackwell.

- McHugh C, Way J (2015). "Broome on Reasoning". *Teorema: Revista Internacional de Filosofía.* 34 (2): 131–140. ISSN 0210-1602. JSTOR 43694673.

- Lee W (2020). "Enkratic Rationality Is Instrumental Rationality". *Philosophical Perspectives.* 34 (1): 164–183.

doi:10.1111/phpe.12136. ISSN 1520-8583.

- Steward H. "Akrasia - Routledge Encyclopedia of Philosophy". www.rep.routledge.com. Retrieved 13 May 2021.
- Tenenbaum S (2010). "Akrasia and Irrationality". A Companion to the Philosophy of Action. Blackwell: 274–282. doi:10.1002/9781444323528.ch35. ISBN 9781444323528.
- McGregor D (1960). The Human Side of Enterprise. New York: McGraw-Hill.
- Malone T (1997). "Is 'Empowerment' Just a Fad? Control, Decision-Making, and Information Technology". Sloan Management Review. 23 (38).
- Markowitz L (1996). "Employee Participation at the Workplace: Capitalist Control or Worker Freedom?". Critical Sociology. 22 (2): 89–103. doi:10.1177/089692059602200205. S2CID 143788356.
- Denison DR (1990). Corporate Culture and Organizational Effectiveness. New York: John Wiley & Sons. ISBN 9780471800217.
- Mayo E (1949). "Hawthorne and the Western Electric Company.". In Pugh DS (ed.). Organization Theory: Selected Readings (Second ed.). New York: Penguin. pp. 279–292.
- Miner JB (September 2003). "The rated importance, scientific validity, and practical usefulness of organizational behavior theories: A quantitative review". Academy of Management Learning & Education. 2 (3): 250–68. doi:10.5465/amle.2003.10932132.
- Pisello T (2 March 2004). "Managing IT According To A Hierarchy Of Needs". WebProNews. Archived from the original on 27 November 2018. "The well-traveled theory by Abraham Maslow asserts that people are motivated by unsatisfied needs [...]."
- "The benefits of a motivated workforce - Motivation". Eduqas - GCSE Business Revision - Eduqas. BBC Bitesize. Retrieved

2020-10-09.

- Goldthorpe JH, Lockwood D, Bechhofer F, Platt J (1968). The affluent worker: Industrial attitudes and behaviour. Cambridge: Cambridge University Press.
- Weightman J (2008). The Employee Motivation Audit. Cambridge Strategy Publications.
- Kenton W. "What Is the Hawthorne Effect?". Investopedia. Retrieved 2020-10-09.
- Vroom V, Lee D (1964). Work and Motivation.
- "Description of a Positive Workplace". Small Business - Chron.com. Retrieved 2020-10-09.
- Burgers C, Eden A, Van Engelenburg MD, Buningh S (2015-07-01). "How feedback boosts motivation and play in a brain-training game". Computers in Human Behavior. 48: 94–103. doi:10.1016/j.chb.2015.01.038. ISSN 0747-5632.
- Bragg T (2 September 2002). "Motivate your employees by offering more interesting, challenging job experiences". Louisville Business First. Retrieved 2020-10-09.
- Hackman JR, Oldham GR (1980). Work Redesign. Upper Saddle River, N.J.: Pearson Education, Inc. pp. 78–80.
- Ormrod JE (2003). Educational Psychology: Developing Learners. Upper Saddle River, N.J.: Merrill/Prentice Hall. ISBN 978-0-13-088716-0. OCLC 49626269.
- Williams RL, Stockdale SL (2004). "Classroom motivation strategies for prospective teachers". The Teacher Educator. 39 (3): 212–230. doi:10.1080/08878730409555342. S2CID 144007655.
- Whyte CB (2007). "An Additional Look at Orientation Programs Nationally- (reprint of 1986 article in same journal)". National Orientation Directors Association Journal. 15 (1): 71–77.
- Vallerand RJ, Pelletier LG, Blais MR, Brière NM, Senecal C, Vallières ÉF (2016). "The Academic Motivation Scale: A

Measure of Intrinsic, Extrinsic, and Amotivation in Education". Educational and Psychological Measurement. 52 (4): 1003–1017. doi:10.1177/0013164492052004025. S2CID 145465675.

- Harter S (1981). "A new self-report scale of intrinsic versus extrinsic orientation in the classroom: Motivational and informational components". Developmental Psychology. 17 (3): 300–312. doi:10.1037/0012-1649.17.3.300.

- Cordova DI, Lepper MR (1996). "Intrinsic motivation and the process of learning: Beneficial effects of contextualization, personalization, and choice". Journal of Educational Psychology. 88 (4): 715–730. doi:10.1037/0022-0663.88.4.715.

- 100.Whyte CB (2018). "Effective Counseling Methods for High-Risk College Freshmen". Measurement and Evaluation in Guidance. 10 (4): 198–200. doi:10.1080/00256307.1978.12022132.

- 101.Lauridsen K, Whyte CB, eds. (1980). An Integrated counseling and Learning Assistance Center. New Directions Sourcebook. Jossey-Bass.

- 102.Sansone C, Morgan C (1992). "Intrinsic motivation and education: Competence in context". Motivation and Emotion. 16 (3): 249–270. doi:10.1007/bf00991654. S2CID 144370965.

- 103.Katz I, Shahar BH (2015). "What makes a motivating teacher? Teacher's motivation and beliefs as predictors of their autonomy-supportive style". School Psychology International. 36 (6): 575–588. doi:Deci EL, Sheinman L, Nezlek JB (1981). "Characteristics of the rewardee and intrinsic motivation of the rewardee". Journal of Personality and Social Psychology. 40 (1): 1–10. doi:10.1037/0022-3514.40.1.1.

- 104.Tharp R, Yamauchi L (2000). "Instructional Conversations in Native American Classrooms. Rural,

Urban and Minority Education". *Journal of Early Education and Family Review*. 7 (5): 33–37.

- 105.McInerney DM, Swisher KG (April 1995). "Exploring Navajo Motivation in School Settings". *Journal of American Indian Education*. 34: 3.
- 106.Pewewardy C (January 2002). "Learning Styles of American Indian/Alaska Native Students: A Review of the Literature and Implications for Practice". *Journal of American Indian Education*. 41 (3): 22–56. JSTOR 24398583.
- 107.Pelletier W (1969). *Childhood in an Indian Village*. Toronto etc.: Institute for Indian Studies. Neewin Publishing.
- 108.Maynard AE (2004). "Cultures of teaching in childhood: formal schooling and Maya sibling teaching at home". *Cognitive Development*. 19 (4): 517–535. CiteSeerX 10.1.1.492.6959. doi:10.1016/j.cogdev.2004.09.005.
- 109.Rogoff B (2011). *Developing Destinies: A Mayan Midwife and Town*. Cambridge: Oxford University Press. ISBN 978-0-19-971780-4.
- 110.Chavajay P, Rogoff B (January 2002). "Schooling and traditional collaborative social organization of problem solving by Mayan mothers and children". *Developmental Psychology*. 38 (1): 55–66. doi:10.1037/0012-1649.38.1.55. PMID 11806702.
- 111.Lillemyr OF, Søbstad F, Marder K, Flowerday T (June 2010). "Indigenous and non-Indigenous primary school students' attitudes on play, humour, learning and self-concept: a comparative perspective". *European Early Childhood Education Research Journal*. 18 (2): 243–267. doi:10.1080/13502931003784396. S2CID 145281027.
- 112.Rogoff B, Paradise R, Arauz RM, Correa-Chavez M, Angelillo C (2003). "Firsthand learning through intent participation". *Annual Review of Psychology*. 54: 175–203. doi:10.1146/annurev.psych.54.101601.145118. hdl:10400.12/

5953. PMID 12499516.

- 113.Rogoff B (2012). "Learning without lessons: Opportunities to expand knowledge". *Infancia y Aprendizaje.* 35 (2): 233–252. doi:10.1174/021037012800217970. S2CID 144442624.

- 114.Ames P (2013). "Learning to be responsible: Young children transitions outside of school". *Learning, Culture and Social Interaction.* 2 (3): 143–154. doi:10.1016/j.lcsi.2013.04.002.

- 115.Gaskins S (2000). "Children's daily activities in a Mayan village: A culturally grounded description". *Cross-Cultural Research.* 34 (4): 375–389. doi:10.1177/106939710003400405. S2CID 144751184.

- 116.Correa-Chávez M, Roberts AL, Pérez MM (2011). Cultural patterns in children's learning through keen observation and participation in their communities. *Advances in Child Development and Behavior.* 40. pp. 209–41. doi:10.1016/b978-0-12-386491-8.00006-2. ISBN 978-0-12-386491-8. PMID 21887963.

- 117.Mejía-Arauz R, Rogoff B, Dexter A, Najafi B (2007). "Cultural variation in children's social organization". *Child Development.* 78 (3): 1001–14. doi:10.1111/j.1467-8624.2007.01046.x. PMID 17517018.

- 118.Ali J, McInerney DM, Craven RG, Yeung AS, King RB (2013). "Socially Oriented Motivational Goals and Academic Achievement: Similarities Between Native and Anglo Americans". *The Journal of Educational Research.* 107 (2): 123–137. doi:10.1080/00220671.2013.788988. S2CID 144741545.

- 119.Paradise R, Rogoff B (2009). "Side by Side: Learning by Observing and Pitching In". *Ethos.* 37: 102–138. doi:10.1111/j.1548-1352.2009.01033.x.

- 120."LIST OF PERSONNEL BEING CONFERRED

GALLANTRY AND DISTINGUISHED AWARDS ON THE OCCASION OF REPUBLIC DAY 2020" (PDF). Press Information Bureau of India. 25 January 2020. Archived (PDF) from the original on 7 August 2021. Retrieved 7 August 2021.

- 121. "Tokyo Olympics 2020: Armyman Neeraj Chopra hailed 'a true soldier' by defence forces after historic gold". Firstpost. 7 August 2021. Archived from the original on 11 August 2021. Retrieved 7 August 2021.
- 122. Shrivastava, Kislaya (11 August 2021). "India's Olympic Gold Medallist Neeraj Chopra Becomes World Number 2 In Men's Javelin Throw". New Delhi, India: NDTV. Retrieved 12 August 2021.
- 123. "Neeraj Chopra makes National Record again". The Times of India. 5 March 2021. Retrieved 7 March 2021.
- 124. "Tokyo Olympics 2020: Neeraj Chopra wins historic Gold in javelin throw, India's first athletics medal in 100 yrs". Mirror Now. The Economic Times. 7 August 2021. Retrieved 16 August 2021.
- 125. Ganguly, Sudipto; Tennery, Amy (7 August 2021). "U.S., India finally get athletics gold, Japan win baseball title". Reuters. Retrieved 15 August 2021.
- 126. "Neeraj CHOPRA | Profile". World Athletics. Archived from the original on 8 August 2021. Retrieved 9 August 2021.
- 127. Philip, Benson (7 August 2021). "Tokyo Olympics: Farmer's son Neeraj Chopra from Khandra village, Haryana ends India's 100-year wait gold in athletics". Lokmat English. Archived from the original on 7 August 2021. Retrieved 8 August 2021.
- 128. Krishnan, Murukesh (7 August 2021). "From 'Subedar Neeraj Chopra' to 'Olympian Neeraj Chopra' – Story of an Indian Army soldier". Times Now. Archived from the original on 7 August 2021. Retrieved 7 August 2021.

- 129.Lovely Professional University to reward it's student Neeraj Chopra with Rs 50 lakh for clinching gold for India at Tokyo Archived 11 August 2021 at the Wayback Machine Times Now. Retrieved 11 August 2021
- 130.Kumar, Amit (12 August 2021). "I was not thinking about Johannes Vetter, but about myself and my throw: Neeraj Chopra". The Times of India. New Delhi. Retrieved 13 August 2021.
- 131.Ghosh, Avijit (4 September 2018). "How a chubby guy became champ". The Times of India. Archived from the original on 23 April 2021. Retrieved 11 August 2021.
- 132.Amsan, Andrew (29 July 2018). "Asian Games: Neeraj Chopra, spearman from Khandra". The Indian Express. Archived from the original on 7 August 2021. Retrieved 7 August 2021.
- 133.Selvaraj, Jonathan (28 February 2016). "India's latest athletics sensation Neeraj Chopra is brimming with natural talent". The Indian Express. Retrieved 15 August 2021.
- 134."National Sports Awards 2018: List of awardees". The Times of India. 25 September 2018. Retrieved 14 August 2021.
- 135."28th NATIONAL JUNIOR ATHLETICS CHAMPIONSHIPS-2012" (PDF). Athletics Federation of India. 2012. Archived (PDF) from the original on 11 August 2021. Retrieved 11 August 2021.
- 136.Sharma, Nitin (7 August 2021). "Former coach recalls the chubby Neeraj Chopra with a notebook, now an Olympic gold medallist". The Indian Express. Archived from the original on 7 August 2021. Retrieved 7 August 2021.
- 137.Rayan, Stan (7 August 2021). "Neeraj Chopra: From chubby kid trying to lose weight to Olympic champion". The Hindu. ISSN 0971-751X. Archived from the original on 7 August 2021. Retrieved 7 August 2021.
- 138. "Neeraj Chopra: I am not going to be content with

Olympic gold and sit on this laurel". ESPN. 10 August 2021. Retrieved 14 August 2021.

- *139."World record holder Neeraj Chopra gets Army job, starts supporting farmer father". The Times of India. 12 March 2017. Archived from the original on 23 January 2018. Retrieved 29 August 2018.*
- *140.Selvaraj, Jonathan (24 July 2016). "Neeraj Chopra creates history to become first Indian world champion in athletics". The Indian Express. Archived from the original on 8 November 2020. Retrieved 11 August 2021.*
- *141.Sura, Ajay (26 July 2016). "Javelin hero Neeraj Chopra to join Indian Army". The Times of India. Archived from the original on 6 September 2018. Retrieved 29 August 2018.*
- *142.Koshie, Nihal (10 July 2017). "Asian Athletics Championship: Slumbering Neeraj Chopra wakes up in time". The Indian Express. Archived from the original on 6 February 2021. Retrieved 9 August 2021.*
- *143."Neeraj Chopra suffers groin injury in Zurich Diamond League Finals". The Indian Express. 25 August 2017. Retrieved 29 August 2021.*
- *144.Koshie, Nihal (22 February 2018). "Neeraj Chopra reboots along the Rhine". The Indian Express. Retrieved 29 August 2021.*
- *145."CWG 2018: Neeraj Chopra wins javelin gold with season-best throw". The Times of India. 14 April 2018. Archived from the original on 23 April 2021. Retrieved 14 April 2018.*
- *146."IAAF Diamond League: Neeraj Chopra breaks his own javelin throw national record again, finishes fourth". Scroll.in. 4 May 2018. Archived from the original on 7 September 2020. Retrieved 4 May 2018.*
- *147.McKay, Duncan (12 August 2018). "India chooses javelin thrower Chopra as flagbearer for 2018 Asian Games*

Opening Ceremony". insidethegames.biz. Archived from the original on 18 November 2020. Retrieved 7 August 2021.

- 148. "Asian Games, Live Updates, Day 9: India's Neeraj Chopra Clinches Gold Medal in Javelin Throw Final". News18. 27 August 2018. Archived from the original on 7 August 2021. Retrieved 27 August 2018.
- 149. "Neeraj Chopra recommended for Rajiv Gandhi Khel Ratna by Athletics Federation of India". India Today. 30 May 2020. Archived from the original on 16 July 2021. Retrieved 16 July 2021.
- 150. Philip, Snehesh Alex (8 August 2021). "With Olympics 'golden throw', Subedar Neeraj Chopra could land promotion in Army". ThePrint. Archived from the original on 8 August 2021. Retrieved 9 August 2021.
- 151. "Raining rewards for Neeraj Chopra: A list of cash awards for Olympic gold medallist". The Indian Express. New Delhi, India. 12 August 2021. Retrieved 13 August 2021.
- 152. "Who is Neeraj Chopra's coach?". olympics.com. 9 August 2021. Retrieved 13 August 2021.
- 153. Gupta, Gaurav (8 August 2021). "Mumbai hand that saved Neeraj Chopra's golden arm". The Times of India. Archived from the original on 10 August 2021. Retrieved 11 August 2021.
- 154. Sharma, Nitin (30 January 2020). "Reading Shiv Khera's book Jeet Aapki and meditation helped Neeraj Chopra during tough times". The Indian Express. Archived from the original on 7 August 2021. Retrieved 7 August 2021.
- 155. Koshie, Nihal (30 November 2019). "Neeraj Chopra no longer training with high-profile coach Hohn". The Indian Express. Archived from the original on 6 April 2020. Retrieved 4 May 2020.
- 156. "Neeraj Chopra's former coach dies, javelin star posts emotional message". India Today. 28 July 2018. Archived

from the original on 29 July 2018. Retrieved 4 May 2020.

- 157."Watch: On this day two years ago, Javelin Thrower Neeraj Chopra became a world junior record holder". Scroll.in. 23 July 2018. Archived from the original on 9 November 2020. Retrieved 4 May 2020.
- 158.Das, Indraneel (7 June 2021). "Javelin thrower Neeraj Chopra flies to Europe, first competition at Lisbon meet". The New Indian Express. Archived from the original on 9 August 2021. Retrieved 9 August 2021.
- 159.Koshie, Nihal (8 August 2021). "Tokyo 2020: Neeraj Chopra soars to end generations of heartache". The Indian Express. Archived from the original on 7 August 2021. Retrieved 8 August 2021.
- 160.Das, Tanmay (8 August 2021). "When Odisha opened its arms to Neeraj & Co amid COVID lockdown". The New Indian Express. Archived from the original on 9 August 2021. Retrieved 9 August 2021.
- 161.Selvaraj, Jonathan (5 March 2021). "Neeraj Chopra's Nordic weapon: Breaker of storms, and national records". ESPN. Archived from the original on 14 May 2021. Retrieved 8 March 2021.
- 162.Das, Indraneel (29 May 2021). "After long wait, Neeraj Chopra gets France visa, to leave soon". The New Indian Express. Archived from the original on 9 August 2021. Retrieved 9 August 2021.
- 163."Neeraj Chopra throws 83.18m to clinch gold in Lisbon". The Times of India. 10 June 2021. Archived from the original on 18 June 2021. Retrieved 8 August 2021.
- 164."I was in training mode in the Lisbon event: Javelin thrower Neeraj Chopra". The New Indian Express. 11 June 2021. Retrieved 9 August 2021.
- 165."Javelin thrower Neeraj Chopra pulls out of Switzerland event to rest ahead of Olympics". The New Indian Express.

29 June 2021. Archived from the original on 9 August 2021. Retrieved 9 August 2021.

- 166."Missed natural feeling of being in world-class event but staying positive: Neeraj Chopra". The New Indian Express. 11 July 2021. Archived from the original on 9 August 2021. Retrieved 9 August 2021.
- 167."Athletics CHOPRA Neeraj – Tokyo 2020 Olympics". Olympics. Archived from the original on 7 August 2021. Retrieved 7 August 2021.
- 168."Tokyo Olympics: Spotlight on javelin thrower Neeraj Chopra to end Independent India's wait for medal in athletics". India Today. 7 August 2021. Archived from the original on 8 August 2021. Retrieved 9 August 2021.
- 169.Selvaraj, Jonathan (7 August 2021). "Ice-cold Neeraj Chopra turns Olympic legend with India's first athletics gold". ESPN. Archived from the original on 7 August 2021. Retrieved 7 August 2021.
- 170."Tokyo 2020: With 7 medals, India records its best-ever Olympic performance". India Today. 7 August 2021.
- 171."Neeraj Chopra Men's Javelin Throw Live Updates, Tokyo Olympics: Neeraj Throws 87.58, 1st on Board in Gold Position". News18. 7 August 2021. Archived from the original on 7 August 2021. Retrieved 7 August 2021.

Notes

www.ingramcontent.com/pod-product-compliance
Lightning Source LLC
Chambersburg PA
CBHW070554160726
48003CB00005B/2041